Fiona Kha

Illustrated by Vidya A
(The Nanda Soobben's Centre for Fine Arts, Animation & Design)

Layout: Summer Designs Tel: (031) 4017703
Printed By: Art Printers Tel: (031) 3094273

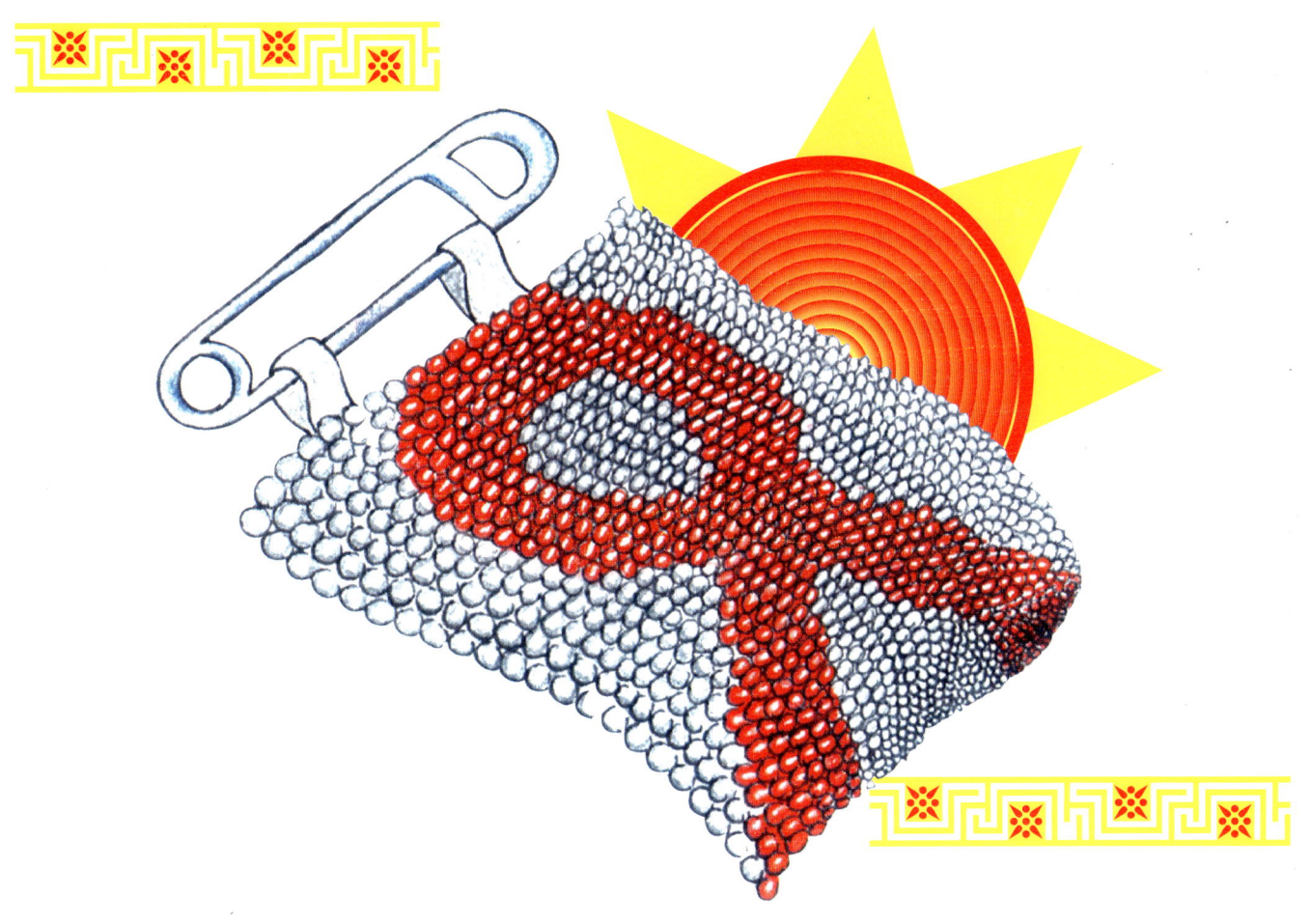

ISBN: 0-620-28835-3
First Edition
First Impression - 2002

No part of this book may be reproduced or transmitted in any form or by any means, electronic, electrostatic, magnetic tape or mechanical including photo-copying, recording or by any information storage and retrieval system, without the exclusive permission in writing from the publisher.

Washesha Publications
Cluster Box 12678, Jura Street, Shallcross 4093.
Cell: 083 699 4667

Hi!
I AM HIV POSITIVE

Acknowledgements:

Mr Aboobaker, The Islamic Medical Association, Linda Hiles of the Nelson Mandela School and Zohra Khan.

I like to thank Ashraf Shahzade, Krish Moodley, Fazila Khan, Mannie Moodley, Deon Chetty, Nanda Soobben, Ismaeel and Fathima Zara.

May God Bless You.

Also Special thanks to my family for their patience and love.

Hi! My name is Thandeka.

My name means' the loved one'.

I live in Umzinto in Kwa - Zulu Natal.

We have a large farm with lots of animals.

We also plant maize, madumbies and green chillies.

Gogo likes to plant nuts.
She pulls them out from under the ground and washes them.
Then, she dries them in the sun.
It is packed in a sack which she places on her head and carries into town where she sells them.
I like living on the farm.
I get to help Gogo with the farming.

She always tells us stories about dog chases and the beautiful madams that live in big houses. Sometimes she jokes about the little children who repeat after her when she calls out,

'Got green chillies Makoti!'

In sunshine or rain, she leaves the farm before dawn. Gogo takes a taxi into town. She only gets back late in the evening when everything is sold. I love Gogo too, because the money she earns, pays for my school fees. We also buy groceries from the supermarket with the money. We love eating the fresh vegetables from our garden.

My Mum is a health worker. She has opened a health care centre in the village. It is called The Gift Of Love, Isiphuthando. I also help mum at the care centre. We asked all the people in the village to help with the painting of the centre. Each one of them drew a picture of their message of love. Mum opened this centre for all the Aids patients. There are many patients who come to the centre for medicines. She gets a lot of help from the local clinic with food and medicines.

The nurses are very helpful and pleasant. Do you know how many people suffer from this disease?
I ask my mum questions all the time. She says a six year old girl should be educated on HIV and Aids.

I am HIV positive!
I have the Aids virus!
I asked Mum how I became infected.
She told me that Dad was HIV positive.
As soon s he heard mum was having a baby,
he left us all alone.
He never came back!

I looked at a chart today that told me all about how the virus enters the body. We all have blood cells in our blood. There are white and red blood cells in our body.

The white blood cells are like soldiers in the body.

They fight any illness (bad germs) and help to keep us strong. When the aids virus HIV enters the body, this virus pretends and acts like a soldier, like a white blood cell.

It pushes its way into the white blood cell eating all the nourishment and strength of the white cell. soon the white cell dies and the HIV cell becomes stronger.

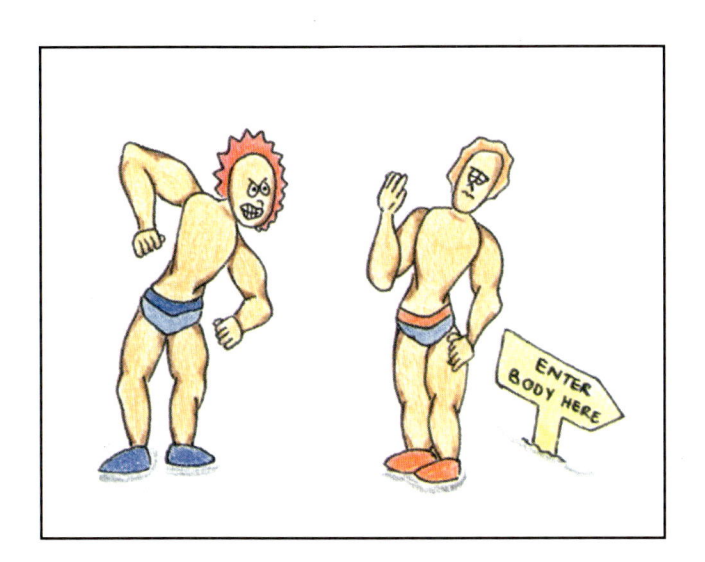

It bursts open and spreading lots of little HIV cells to all parts of the body

Soon the body becomes very weak from the virus.

Mum says that if we live a healthy lifestyle,
we can live a very long time.
We must eat fresh fruit and vegetables.

Adults should not drink and smoke and we must exercise.

There are many people who do not like people who are HIV positive.
They feel they will catch the disease.

We can share cups and plates, toilets and bathrooms.
We can hug and be loved as well as give love.

This is why my mum called the care centre Gift of Love.
It is priceless and it is one of the most precious things in our lives.

This virus stays in our body fluids.
So, unless you come into contact with an infected person's body fluid like blood or semen you cannot be infected.
The virus does not last long outside the body fluid.
It dies!

I do feel sick on some days.
The Nursing Sister comes from the clinic to visit me.
She brings some medicines to help me feel better.

Many of the people who are dying love to remember the days when they were younger and healthier.
I help them make memory boxes.
In these memory boxes we place old photographs of friends, family and also achievements.

Sometimes they go to new places or on holiday and take pictures.
Looking at these pictures make them smile as they always remember something funny or exciting.
Many of them write letters that they would like to leave to their children or little cards which I help them make.
We use dried flowers, ribbon or beads.

Mrs Masimola comes to the centre once a week.
She teaches the Aids patients beadwork.
They make badges with the Aids logo.

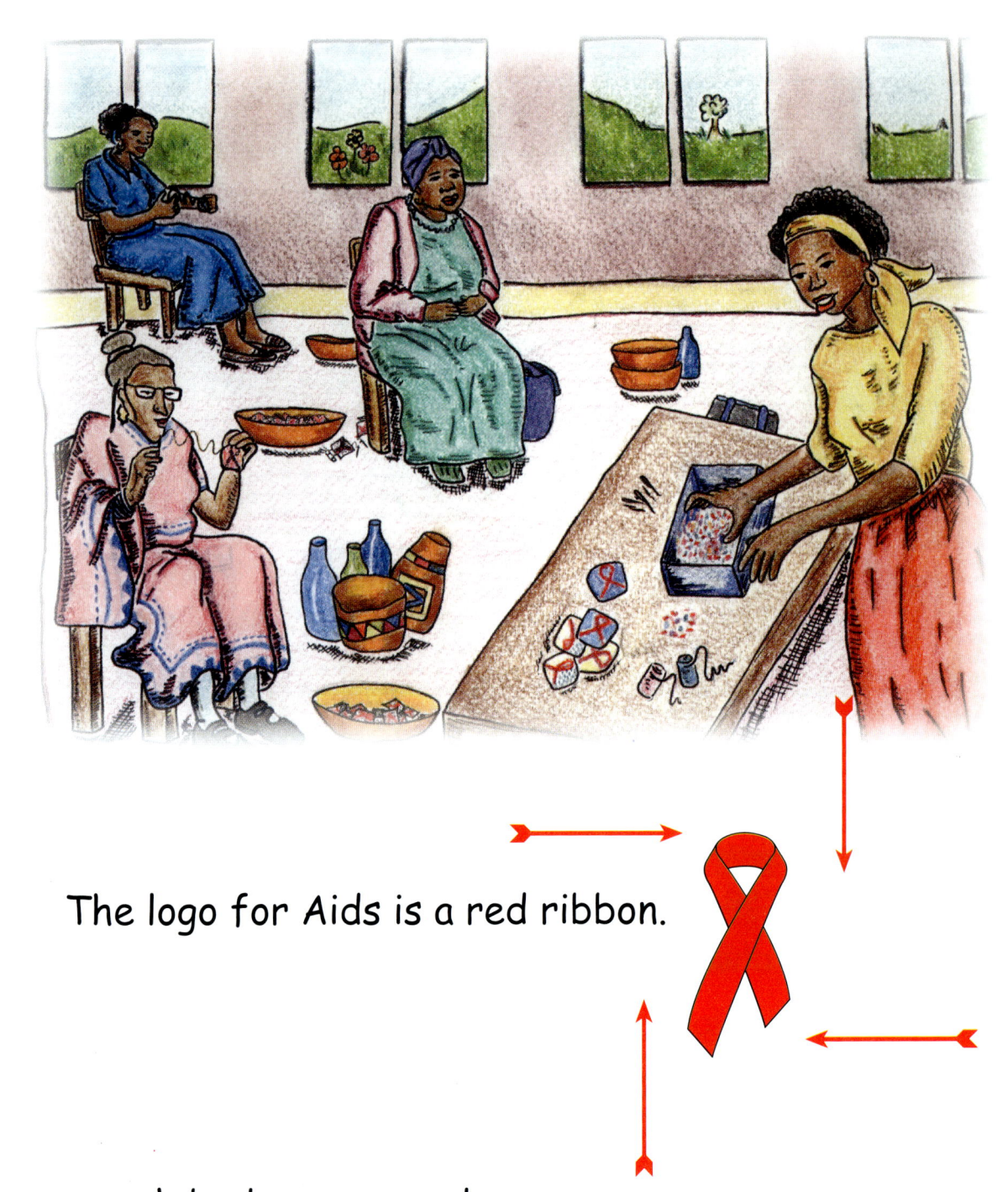

The logo for Aids is a red ribbon.

When enough badges are made,
the ladies take them into the town to sell them.
They use this money for their food.
They also make necklaces and bracelets.

Most of the people who are HIV positive are unemployed. People are still not educated about Aids. They feel if you are HIV positive and you work with them they can get Aids from you.

Mum and Mrs Masimola wrote many letters to the government asking for assistance.
She is still waiting for the reply.
There are also many mothers who are having babies that come to the centre.

There are no drugs for them
to take to prevent the babies
from getting the virus.
When the babies are born,
I love playing with them.
They are small and very cute.
They smell fresh with baby powder.

5 Feb 2002

Letter to the South African Government

Dear Mr. President

The Gift of Love requires assistance desperately. Please send people to help urgently.

Many thanks
Mrs Masimola

When the patients are very
ill and cannot come to the care centre,
Mum and I do home visits. We always take them something special. This puts a smile on their face.

ATTITUDES.

I was walking down the street, when the other children called on their dog to bite me because they all knew I was HIV positive.

They were rude to Mum,
calling her names,
telling her that she deserved it.
One day a man threw a stone at my Mum.

People stopped inviting us to their homes and if we went
to visit, they just closed the doors on our faces.
I have also had the children spit on my face.
None of them will play with me at school,
nor would sit next to me.

Now, there are members of their family who come to the centre.
They have the Aids virus.
I give them fresh porridge to drink and fresh fruit to eat.
Some of them are very poor.
These boys and girls are very quiet now.
They know what they were doing was wrong.
They also know that anyone can get Aids.
I talk to them about Aids.

Mum is very brave. She is invited to schools and colleges to talk openly about HIV Aids.
She shows them the use of condoms and talks to children about their bodies.

It is very important to be clean at all times. Sometimes the children laugh because they are very shy, but they always learn something new.

She shows them parts of their bodies and name the different parts.

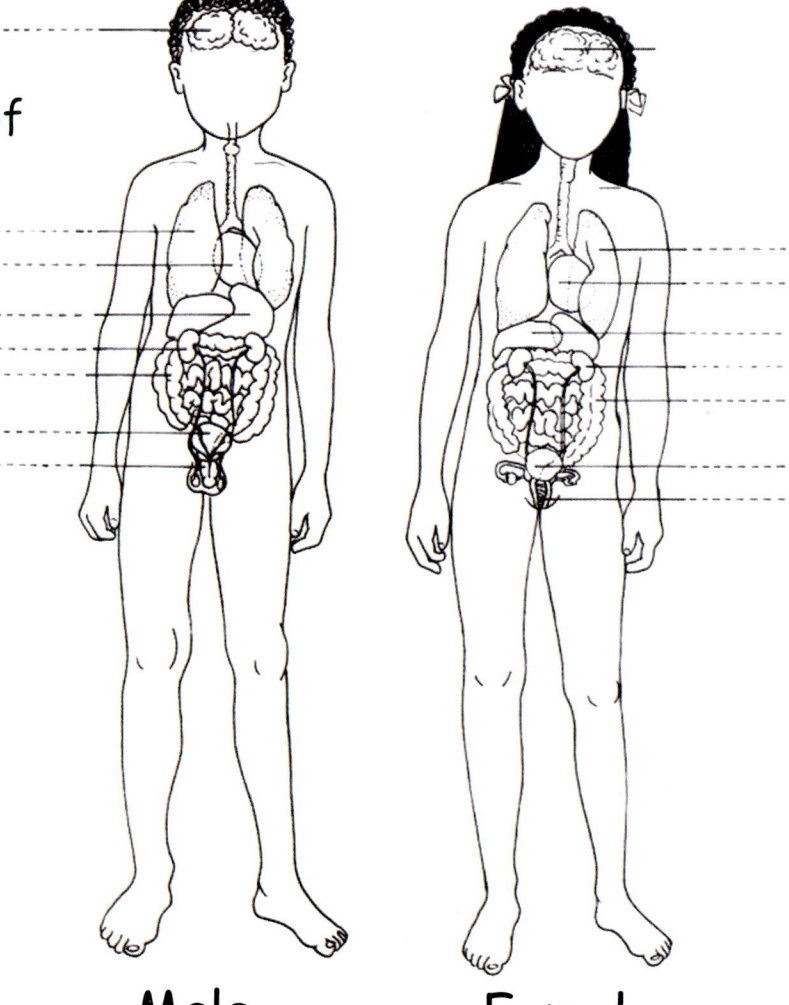

Male   Female

Mum also tells them about drug abuse and getting Aids by abusing drugs, sharing needles and that their lives are very precious. To value their lives they must not take drugs and they must leave sex for after marriage.

She also teaches us about knowing our bodies and not letting anyone touch parts of our bodies.
My dolls are used to show us the good touches and the bad touches.

Mum tells the teachers that if anyone of us are injured and there is blood on the wound, then they must take precautions. These are called universal precautions.

The teacher must put a rubber glove or plastic packet on her hand before she touches blood.
She can become infected if there is a cut or wound on her hand.

Now, I think I am very lucky.
If I was not HIV positive I would no meet so many people.
I would not be able to be a part of their lives or touch their lives in some special way.
They make me feel better.

They also make me feel like I have made the most wonderful difference in my life.

I am positive!